LA GRANGE
PUBLIC LIBRARY
10 West Cossitt Avenue
La Grange, IL 60525
lagrangelibrary.org 708.352.0576

DEMCO

Versed

Wesleyan Poetry

RECENT BOOKS BY RAE ARMANTROUT

Next Life (Wesleyan University Press)
Collected Prose (Singing Horse Press)
Up to Speed (Wesleyan University Press)
Veil: New and Selected Poems (Wesleyan University Press)
The Pretext (Green Integer Books)
True (Atelos Publishing Project)

VERSED

Rae Armantrout

Wesleyan University Press

Middletown, Connecticut

Published by Wesleyan University Press, Middletown, CT 06459
www.wesleyan.edu/wespress

© 2009 by Rae Armantrout

First Wesleyan paperback 2010
Printed in the United States of America   5   4   3   2

ISBN for the paperback edition: 978-0-8195-7091-8
ISBN for the cloth edition: 978-0-8195-6879-3

Library of Congress Cataloging-in-Publication Data

Armantrout, Rae, 1947-
  Versed / Rae Armantrout.
    p. cm. — (Wesleyan poetry)
  ISBN 978-0-8195-6879-3 (cloth : alk. paper)
  I. Title.
  PS3551.R455V47 2009
  811'.54—dc22   2008043809

NATIONAL
ENDOWMENT
FOR THE ARTS
A great nation
deserves great art.

This project is supported in part by an award from
the National Endowment for the Arts

Wesleyan University Press is a member of the Green Press Initiative. The paper
used in this book meets their minimum requirement for recycled paper.

Contents

Dark Matter

Acknowledgments

These poems have appeared in the following anthologies and magazines. The author wants to thank their editors.

ANTHOLOGIES: *American Hybrid*. New York: Norton, 2009 (ed. Cole Swenson and David St. John). *The Best American Poetry of 2007*. New York: Scribner, 2007 (ed. Heather McHugh). *The 2008 Rhysling Anthology: The Best Science Fiction, Fantasy, and Horror Poetry of 2008*. Temple City, Calif.: The Science Fiction Poetry Association, 2008 (ed. Drew Morse).

MAGAZINES: *American Poet, American Poetry Review, Chicago Review, Coconut, Colorado Review, Columbia Poetry Review, Conjunctions, Critical Quarterly, Effing, Fence, Fulcrum, The Green Integer Review, The Hat, Jubilat, The Laurel Review, Mark(s), Mi-Poesias, The Nation, The New Yorker, The New Review, No, Origin* (online), *Pequod, Poetry, Tin House, War and Peace: the Future, 26*.

I acknowledge, with thanks, the support of the Guggenheim Foundation and the Foundation for Contemporary Arts for the fellowships I received while finishing this book.

Results

1

Click here to vote
on who's ripe
for a makeover

or takeover

in this series pilot.

Votes are registered
at the server
and sent back

as results.

2

Click here to transform

oxidation
into digestion.

From this point on,
it's a lattice
of ends
disguised as means:

the strangler fig,

the anteater.

3

I've developed the ability
to revise
what I'm waiting for

so that letter
becomes dinner
gradually

while the contrapuntal
nodding
of the Chinese elm leaves

redistributes
ennui

The self-monitoring function
of each cell
"writ large,"

personified ——
a person.

                *

The "Issues of the Day"
are mulled steadily
by surrogates.

                *

Metaphor forms
a crust
beneath which
the crevasse
of each experience.

                *

Traversed
by robotic surveyors.

                *

Mother yells, "Good job!"
when he drops the stick,

"Good job!"
when he walks in her direction

Fetch

1

Was it a flaming mouse
that burned Mares' house down
or was it just the wind?

On Tuesday Mares and his nephew
stood by the original version.

Is this plausible?

Fire Chief Chavez said Tuesday
that he thought so.

2

Let's see

your itty-
bitten specificity
fetish,

your mom's phantasmic
what's-it

held conspicuously
under threat.

Day hoists its mesh
of near
approximations,

(its bright
skein of pores.)

Eyes fetch thrown
shadows

Address

The way my interest
in their imaginary
kiss

is secretly addressed
to you.

＊

Without intention

prongs of ivy
mount the posts
supporting the freeway.

It would be possible to say
each leaf

circumscribes hope

or that each leaf,
fastidiously coming
to one point,

suggests a fear
of the unknown.

＊

These glossy,
laced-up, high-heel boots

(each leaf)

addressed to you

Vehicles

Pairing matched fragments,
then pausing —

archly? ——

Mozart creates a universe
out of pleasantries.

"How is everything
for you today?"

the hostess
at the front desk asks.

    *

If *that* (head-on car-crash)
had happened, we say,

all this
would not have been —

like "having been"
were a lasting thing:

the small tree
on the highway meridian

having been lit up
for a moment now

by sun breaking through cloud

    *

Look how
we "attempted to express ourselves."

Every one of these words is wrong.

It wasn't us.
Or we made no real attempt.
Or there is no discernible difference
between self and expression.

＊

What was meant by "streamlining"
we might guess,

but what was meant by streamlining
as value added
to this

already bulky,
even bulbous,

baby-pink conveyance,

we can only ask

A Resemblance

As a word is
mostly connotation,

matter is mostly
aura?

Halo?

(The same loneliness
that separates me

from what I call
"the world.")

     *

Quiet, ragged
skirt of dust

encircling a ceramic
gourd.

     *

Look-alikes.

"Are you happy now?"

     *

Would I like
a vicarious happiness?

Yes!

Though I suspect
yours of being defective,

forced

Outer

Dolls as celebrities (Barbie);
celebrities as dolls.

I'm the one who can't know if the scraggly old woman
putting a gallon of vodka in her shopping cart feels
guilty, defiant, or even glamorous as she does so. She
may imagine herself as an actress playing an alcoholic
in a film.

Removal activates glamour?

To see yourself as if from the outside — though not as
others see you.

Carried by light,
images remain

while sensation
is so evanescent

as to be always beyond
belief.

The outer world means
State Farm Donuts Tae Kwando?

Thoughts as spent fuel rods.

Preceded and
followed by
statuesque
shadows of cacti
on a lawn.

Today could be described as a retired man humming
tunelessly to himself.

When I ask what you're thinking, you say "about ex-
plaining to children the best way to build a Maypole."

Relations

"Head" and "Bring."

I remember the words.

"Bobble" and "Bauble,"

"Rosy" and "Lonely"

set off now.

What will you
little chimes
bring me?

Time flows
because no set
of proofs

can be complete.
Bring me the friendship

between solving
and dissolving.

Babel

"Let us go down and confuse
their language

so we may distinguish
the people
from our thoughts."

*

Can it be true
that the baby is afraid

his wish
to gobble us up

has been realized
already?

*

Hard to say
since we've thrown our voice

into the future
    and the past

Operations

This child fights cancer
with the help
of her celebrity fan club,

says,
"Now I know how hard it is
to be a movie star."

*

"Hey,
my avatar's not working!"

*

This small hawk on a wire
above tangled flowers.

*

Speech, too, was thought
to be inhabited
by a god.

Then hunger
invented light.

Help

Creased, globular,
shiny, baby

pumpkins on stalks
upright in a vase.

Let amorphous

restlessness condense
to objects like these

again.

    *

A space
"inside"

can't bear
to be un-

interrupted.

I mark it:

"I" "I" "I"

    *

If this were a stutter
of brittle reeds,

an evening glint
fingering each

"at a time"

might help

Name Calling

Objects are *silly*.

Lonesome

as the word "Ow!"

is.

     *

Could we grant them
a quorum —

dense,

with the shiny
glossolalia
of the leaves,

the resilience
of open-ended
questions?

     *

Bud-nipped.

What the pudendum
attempts
to pinch off,

tries repeatedly.

What comes to
be called pleasure

Pleasure

A sleight-of-hand
equilibrium

being produced
as bees

pass one another,

a ticklish rumble
shuttling between blooms.

I'd like to think
I'm one,

no,
all of them.

*

This sense of
my senses

being *mine*
is what passes

life to life?

How distinguish one
light from the next?

Only distinctions *can*
matter.

(Canned matter.)

*

Just made up
                    of
tuning fork ferns,

blackbird pipe-lettes:

little golden
self-measuring
extents

Guess

The jacaranda, for instance, is beautiful
but not serious.

That much
I can guess.

And that the view
is softened by curtains.

That the present moment
is an exception,

is the queen bee
a hive serves,

or else an orphan.

So the jacaranda
is foreign and extravagant.

It gestures in the distance.

Between there and here
you ask

what game
we should play next week.

So we'll be alive
next week,

continuing
what you may or may not

mean to be
an impossible flirtation

Locality

1

"Is it nummy? Yeah, huh?"

2

Songs as empathy
evacuation engines.

It's not that I wish
to pledge slavish devotion
as the singer seems to do;

it's not that I want to be
the object of such attention —
but I'll listen to this song

again and again.

3

Where you put them —

did you, for instance,

those window bars

reflected

in sun glasses

upside down

between remotes?

4

Wires dip obligingly
between blanched poles,
slightly askew.

Any statement I issue,
if particular enough,

will prove
I was here

Wannabe

Impossibly teetering
is one way
to remain.

Half contemptuous, half
ravished

by vampire wannabes
maybe.

*

A two-lane highway
between ghost-towns —

one of the clichés
you love

the memory, not
of events

but of continuity
itself.

*

Who *are* you anyway?

Stretch

Lime green
against dark foliage,
the Emerald Oil sign
gleams alone.

Stars slingshot
round the center
at millions of miles per.

In rest home beds, patients
hang on
as if to love.

Moment to
moment's stretched
plausibility.

(Body beneath
 a wooden plank,

she's sucking her
grandmother's cock.)

Left Behind

To reinvent
anomalous figments.

Twisted and white, limbs
strike poses.

One ballerina after another
on point
down the highway meridian —

eucalyptus

committed to attitudes
just so

but still awash
in their own
equivocal leaf shadow.

I pass as if to pass
were to think better of something.

2

Dreams unspool
contexts

with an ersatz
tongue-in-cheek

familiarity, conspicuously
flimsy:

a singer intoning "Venice Boulevard"
on a store sound system
late last night,

a crooner placing us
perhaps among flight students —
reminiscing,

"when you're land-ing
on Highway Fi-ive"

Amplification

Some think
in the first days

Hunger and Lust
arose separately
and then paired up by chance

having only
self-love in common —

and what is that?

Still, what a pair they've been!

*

Some think we can
achieve escape velocity

if only we can make
our thoughts bounce

harder and harder off
the near walls —

the limits —
of what is known,

what is trite
about these characters.

*

We have it
on good authority

that we're dying
to express this

one thousand times more
or less precisely,

dying to practice

Bonding

On the television in an empty pharmacy,
the contestant
whose guess is closest
to retail
squeals.

*

A want,
conceived as illusory

(rhetorical),
is said

to underlie the real,
underwrite matter.

*

A man tells a camera
he prefers "lady-boys"
because they can't fake orgasm.

*

In the updraft,
the particulate
glitz
is beside itself.

*

Check-plus! I wait
for my thought
to reappear.

(I trust recognitions.)

*

Pathos
of strangers' headlights
tracing the curve at dusk

is inexplicable

Through

1

The intentions come
previously.

Little apron leaves,

what are you
covering up,

plump

and forgotten on a
woody stalk?

Will itself,

 unoccupied,

                    unowned

2

These dark tunnels
into

and through
the loving look.

Reaching both
and neither

always makes me hot.

"Did you have fun
playing with trains,

Phantom Stallion,

Rainbow Frog?"

Scumble

What if I were turned on by seemingly innocent words
such as "scumble," "pinky," or "extrapolate?"

What if I maneuvered conversation in the hope that
others would pronounce these words?

Perhaps the excitement would come from the way the
other person touched them lightly and carelessly with
his tongue.

What if "of" were such a hot button?

"Scumble of bushes."

What if there were a hidden pleasure
in calling one thing
by another's name?

Worth While

A rod: a list,

a mop-top palm
cut-out
against sunset,

chocolate
pastries in the shape
of pyramids,

an elderly, bent figure
beneath a feathered Stetson.

*

Terri fears
she may be risking her job
as an afterlife consultant.

Melinda is comforted by Jed
when she twists her ankle trying
to evade an angry ghost.

Unanswered questions
change things
between Booth and Bone.

*

A string of raindrops
dangling
from an iron bar reveals
opportunities for
clarity.

At the breakfast table,
Mary's dead parents

become impatient
when she counts the wad
of small denomination bills
they presented her with
on her birthday.

Dilation

Pupils fixed

on the "It Girl's"
production

of fame's emptiness.

A surface
comprised of flicker
and twinge.

Lapsing circles
stripe

the pool's vacant blue

as I might

               what?
They are

going off
in this

long instance

Inscription

God
as the lace-making
machine,

the hypnotized spider.

Why shouldn't
an idée fixe
be infinite?

Blithering symmetries.

More of you are coming.

     *

"I think our incentives
are sexy and edgy."

     *

As if you
could become another person
by setting off
an automatic
cascade of responses
in his/her body.

As if you could escape
by following

the path you carved
there

to its prescribed end.

*

Poems addressed
to their own dead letters —
campy femme-fatales.

Poems addressed
to their end-times'
desiccation.

Entropy increases as I recall
less and less
of the number string.

Snackle-crackle
of strings breaking —
that radiation hiss evening things out.

*

Look — I'm cooperating!
I can pull myself apart
and still speak

Either Side

Proscenium of nearly identical mountain ridges, arched
out and downward, one "after" another, to the valley
floor: curtains tied back, a gesture

*

Skin falling into pleats around my lower jaw as my head
bends forward

*

Glassy, copper inlets
leading "off"
into mist
between pairs, sets
of small, long-treed islands
make gorgeous —
because empty? —
promises

*

The short moan — or hum? —
you exhale
as you drift toward sleep
is an island
I can't visit

Equals

1

As if, after all,

the thing that comes to mind
squared
times inertia

equaled the "real."

2

One lizard
jammed headfirst

down the throat
of a second.

New Genres

1

A witness claims to have seen a spirit. From this premise,
a ragged band sets out,
tramping through an old house in the dark,
joking or bickering,
carrying equipment meant to measure "fluctuations."
The existence of the spirit
should remain an open —
so foreclosed —
question.

2

Pockets of self-reference arise. As if I
could read the mind of the creator,
I already see that the father
is the stalker
he pursues
and, eventually,
neutralizes

Presto

"Breaking
Anna Nicole news

as she buries
her son."

*

"What do you want
to be?"

Skeleton suits
and Superman outfits —

inappropriate touching
on drugstore racks.

*

Presto!

Pairs of flies
re-tie

the old knot
mid-air.

*

Blonde wigs and
wizard caps.

"I want to go back!"

Invisible knot.

I want to be that!

Decor

Drinking tea to pass time;
growing leaves to pass time.

Concrete wall —
the arm slung round this
café patio — is studded
with uneven stones.

2

Ground cover of pert
green hearts:

mass market.

And these hot-pink,
splay-petalled pinwheels —

such toss-offs!

3

Already
it's started again

with new bodies
inflected differently

so that most of us
will end up loving

some dated version,

feeling shame

New

If yellow
is the new black,

the new you
is a cartoon

spokesman
who blows his lines

around bumptious 3-D
Hondas,

apologizes often,
and remains cheerful.

*

The new pop song
is about getting real:

"You had a bad day.
The camera don't lie."

But they're lying
to you
about the camera.

*

Since Fallujah
is the new Antigua,

sunlight nibbles
on pre-
charred

terrain
in the electric fireplace.

Heaven

1

It's a book
full of ghost children,

safely dead,

where dead means
hidden,

or wanting
or not wanting

to be known.

2

Heaven is symmetric
with respect to rotation.

It's beautiful
when one thing changes

while another thing
remains the same.

3

Fading redundancies.

Feathery runs.

Alternate wisps.

Imaginary

sprung striations.

"Imaginary" meaning
"seen by humans."

Lengths

1

Evening succeeds evening.

Demons discourse
on familiar topics.

They describe a wraith's response
to a description.

"I think he was signaling."

One night
differs from all other nights

through their deployment
of synonyms.

"Craft a way forward."

"Get out ahead
of this
with his plan."

2

Aren't you exhausted,

you green spear, you
peel-back purple?

All divided
column,

all split hair,

mirrored and re-
counted for.

You've been crossing
every
with *only*,

going to any
mandible
or bud

Just

A confidential twinkle

from the spun bead
or leaf

seen
by everyone

"through all eternity" —

though "now"

is always just beginning.

   *

I'm composed largely
of what the streets and rooms
look like,

of *how* to arrive
just here.

(Heaven
as default position.)

Tiny, intense,
multiple

clusters
of purple verbena

Oh Princess,
you apple-core afloat

in coke
in a Styrofoam cup,
on an end-table,

you dust, glass, book, crock, thorn, moon.

Oh Beauty who fell asleep
on your birthday,

we swipe at you.

                *

How are we defining "dream?"

An exaggerated sense

of the relevance
of these details,

of "facts"
as presented?

A peculiar
reluctance to ask

presented by whom
and in what space?

                *

By space we mean
the collapsible

whirligig
of attention,

the figuring and
reconfiguring

of charges

among orbits
          (obits)
that has taken forever

The Catch

Cirrus fringes
ring the horizon.

"Where two or more
are gathered . . ."
Name, name, name.

*

They
will be — are —
together *still*
somewhere in time;

they won't be
together *again*

though "again" is
what they always
want

Running

Let's say the universe
is made of strings
that "vibrate" or thrash
in an effort

to minimize the area
that is the product
of their length
and their duration in time.

*

Let's call contraction
"focus"
or "pleasure."

*

You'll step forward,
I know,

into the contracting
light

ready to like
anyone.

How far will you get?

You'll be far ahead
and distracted.

By what?

I won't see it.

I'll be running to catch up.

I'll know you
by your willingness.

I won't believe

that what's continual
is automatic

Later

1

To be beautiful
and powerful enough
for someone
to want to break me

          up

into syndicated ripples.

Later I'll try
to rise from these dead.

2

How much would this body
have had to be otherwise in order
not to be mine,

for this world
not to exist?

When would that difference
have had to begin?

3

The old lady invited me to her soirée. Maybe I was even
older than she was. I was mysterious, at any rate, a rarity,
until the room filled up. Then not. When she handed
out chocolates, she forgot me. I gesticulated as if it were
funny and she gave me two pink creams. Me! As if I
would have ever wanted these!

4

They drive me
out to sea.

Secretly, I am still
_____, the mysterious.

I speak in splashes.

Later
I have the lonely dream

Own

Woman in a room near mine moans, "I'm dying. I want
to be fine. It's my body!
Don't let me! Don't touch me!"

*

By definition,
I'm the blip
floating across my own
"field of vision . ."

*

On closed eyes I see the spartan wall of the ICU
covered in a scrambled hodge-podge of sticky notes,
crossing one another at all angles,
illegibly written over, snippets of reference,
madly irrelevant.

*

Symbolism as the party face of paranoia.

Chorus of expert voices beyond my door, forever
dissecting my case.

"But the part is sick
of representing the whole."

*

"We will prevail,"
says the leader on multiple
screens. The words
are empty, but he's there
inside the lie
everyone believes —

that nothing
will really change. He's become pure
being, insisting
only on insistence.

*

A crowd (scene) of cells, growing wildly,
by random access to stock types,
(Play any role you like and go on
forever. Who is speaking?)
Able to draw blood vessels to itself
by emitting a mock distress call.

*

From deep time,
patterns
on my grandmother's crockery
rise
to cover my closed eyelids,
lumpy fruits and flowers, brown
against a cream background.

*

Dream that Aaron is telling friends to be quiet because
he's listening to a rumble, a white noise voice from his
own intestines which he believes is telling him how to
save me. "SHH!" he says to anyone who speaks.

Birth Order

1

You're it.

It is (you are)
an error

with an arsenal
of disguises,

with a system
of incorporation
built in,

with enmity,

with direction.

2

What have you got to lose?

This
gray tile roof,

gray sky scored
by power lines.

This framed measure
of distance
as intimacy.

Shadows of fingers
(mine)
move across the white page.

Anyone
could write this.

That word —
"this" —

firstborn,
unnecessary

Together

Now I am always perched on a metal examination table.
Two people, a doctor and a nurse, come at intervals
to tell me whether I will live or die. They do this with
practiced solemnity. They're smug or snug in their
habits, their relative safety, of course, but that is to be
expected. And I wait expectantly, even eagerly, as if I
might be of some help. If the news is bad, I imagine,
they will direct our attention to an area of concern. For
a moment, we will lean together toward that place.

On Your Way

On your way to The Sea of Reeds you will meet the
Soul Devouring Demon. You've heard it all before
and you believe it. Why not? Why would they lie? You
must wear the beetle amulet to avoid being consumed.
But it's also true that you can't really know until it's
actually happening. So you have a sort of knowledge
which, even if later confirmed in each detail, is still
not real knowledge. He will weigh your heart and,
if it's too heavy, you'll be swallowed up. What is this
extra element that is mingled in when you arrive at the
ordained spot?

Translation

The thing that makes us human,

monkey-see, monkey-do speed-up,

a "call to mimesis,"

now comes from everywhere at once.

*

The cumulus

and the white flash

from under

the mocking-bird's wing

make what?

*

Repeat wake measurement.

"Check to see"

"Check to see,"

birds say,

"that enough time

has passed."

Around

Time is pleased
to draw itself
                    out,
permit itself
pendulous loops,

to allow them
meaning,

this meaning,

as it goes

              along.

              *

Chuck and I are pleased
to have found a spot
where my ashes can be scattered.
It looks like a construction site
now
but it's adjacent
to a breathtaking, rocky coast.
Chuck sees places
where he might snorkel.
We're being shown through
by a sort of realtor.
We're interested but can't get her
to fix the price.

              *

"The future
is all around us."

It's a place,

anyplace
where we don't exist.

Dark Matter

1

Who am I
to experience a burst
of star formation?

I know this —

after the first rush
of enthusiasm

any idea
recedes and dims.

2

Each one
is the inverse
shape of what's
missing.

3

One might try
summing
the matter up

in a single
Judas kiss,

all bitter-sweet
complicity

and feigned ignorance

Unbidden

The ghosts swarm.
They speak as one
person. Each
loves you. Each
has left something
undone.

*

Did the palo verde
blush yellow
all at once?

Today's edges
are so sharp

they might cut
anything that moved.

*

The way a lost
word

will come back
unbidden.

You're not interested
in it now,

only
in knowing
where it's been.

Had

1

And so I ask,
"Do you need both
skies?"

I say keep
"jets" and "its"
consistent.

I suggest
again
that you strip down
while remaining calm

2

It may be that
reclining
lessens the pressure

(or presence),

but there are still
sensations

to be considered,

no, not "considered,"
dealt with,

no, not "dealt with"
either,

had, perhaps,

but with no rights
of possession,

no sense
of constituting
past

Simple

for Aaron Korkegian

Complex systems can arise
from simple rules.

It's not
that we *want* to survive,
it's that we've been drugged
and made to act
as if we do

while all the while
the sea breaks
and rolls, painlessly, under.

If we're not copying it,
we're lonely.

Is this the knowledge
that demands to be
passed down?

Time is made from swatches
of heaven and hell.

If we're not killing it,
we're hungry.

In Place

1

We've been seated
in the afterlife.

Here
it's a good night
when the impala sprints off,

a good night
when the pride rips
at the carcass.

2

"Be the one, be the one,
be the one,"

pulses

from the four corners
of Starbucks.

3

At bottom,

where position
joins conjecture,

we *posit*.

We stand
on one foot,

swaying

in fresh fog.

Music

Still the run-up
to the primaries.

Hot searches:

tiger attack,
polar bears.

Nothing.

Or a hint
of bitters
at the scoured edge.

Three piccolo notes
from the bushes.

A snatch
of music. Call it
that.

Perfect

Perfect red roses
coaxed
to frame a door

beyond which
a couple bickers —

and why not?

*

Dusty webs — yes!

A ray of sun
touches a hill

and I understand
the noise
faces make.

*

In paradise
where "is"
is different,

where tangled
white knots
at the end of a rug

are also some bright
curls of surf

Whatever

Up and down

the branch

she's twelve,

she's waking up

to herself,

opening

her pairs of

stubby, yellow

wings.

＊

It starts off with innocent,
endless iterations,

twitters — whatever.

But the devil says
boring.

The devil says faster,
change it up.

What's the matter?

As if this were a matter
of life and death

and now it is.

Now they're chasing us
down a twisting
trunk — whatever.

Now we're chasing them.

Solution

A solution is found
when creatures
from the last ice age
band together
to survive.

Circumstances spin
like the mobile
above a baby crib.

Follow along
with an endearing
first person,

a penguin.

You won't get far.

You're the thing
that waits

to trap
each passing thought,

the anxious
blank
that God loves.

Resounding

Are you still interested
in the image

of this island
as a brown shoulder

or breast

half-hidden
by clouds?

Are you turned on
by chimeras?

The impossible woman,

part igneous,
part surge.

               *

Go be
embedded,

beaded, pebbled.

The fickle luster.
That's right.

The fretwork
of disaster.

Go on be
half

shrouded by

Like

1

She never said, "Look at that bush" or "Look at the sea;
that's a beautiful bruise-blue perpetually subsiding." She
drew my attention to only a few things: Xmas lights, The
Last Days, Frontier Land.

2

"What it's like
to be me."

Where watch out
and report back
cross —

a stubborn eddy.

A tendency
to take exception?

How much of *me*
could be lost
while *like* remained?

Could *like* stand alone?

Does it?

Poem

Attention wanes.

The ability
to arrive

from scattered locations
at one time,

making a picture appear,
wanes.

    *

In your dream we're in a far off land
and I look completely different,

indifferent,

pretending not
to recognize you.

But here I hold
your dream
in my poem.

Djinn

Haunted, they say, believing
the soft, shifty
dunes are made up
of false promises.

Many believe
whatever happens
is the other half
of a conversation.

Many whisper
white lies
to the dead.

"The boys are doing really well."

Some think
nothing is so
until it has been witnessed.

They believe
the bits are iffy;

the forces that bind them,
absolute.

The Racket

1

It's as if
the real
thing —
your own
absence —
can never be
uncovered.

2

Each actor's face
seems to have survived
the same brave battle

to remain in character.
They're posed
on the rubble

used to indicate
the past.

It turns out
this is heaven.

3

In the present

cancer sets up
a free market
in your gut.

The fog lifts
and the birds start in.

Each works
to replace itself
with a bit of racket.

Provenance

It's characteristic of X
to place his anxiety here

between "time"
and "alive."

What can you give me
for this glimpse
and its provenance?

I've got one just like it.

What interests me now
are spin-offs
of spin-offs.

The narrative
that rescues us
once more

in a less probable way.

By sailing
upside down at dusk
we've returned
from the land of the dead.

AMERICA

The playboy scion of a weapons company repents. His company, he sees now, is corrupt, his weapons being sold (behind his back) to strong men. Alone, he builds a super weapon in the shape of a man. Now, more powerful and more innocent than ever before, he attacks.

HAPPENING

The train halts. An engineer tells us we're stopped because we've lost touch with the outside world. Things are happening ahead, but we don't know what they are. *This* could represent an act of war. We stand in a field, no longer passengers.

God and Mother
went the same way.

    *

What's a person to us
but a contortion
of pressure ridges
palpable
long after she is gone?

    *

A thin old man in blue jeans,
back arched, grimaces
at the freezer compartment.

    *

Lying in the tub,
I'm telling them —

the missing persons —

that a discrepancy
is a pea

and I am a Princess.

The Line

The eye skirts the tree,
the roof, the power line
and doubles back.

This precedes narrative
and this is what remains of it.

The eye pivots,
feigns interest,

then follows a strand
of metal beads

down to the sweet
faux bell
of the pull.

*

On screen

the wide eye
of the shriveled man

stands for "More!" and
stands for "No!"

Slip

1

As if we know
what *bliss* is,

this lozenge
dissolves,

purple and pink,
a warm largesse,

into the cool sea.

2

I want to catch
myself

if only
in the wrong

as if in the nude
in a recurring dream.

Hey

1

Sound
may be addressed
                    to you
or it may not.

2

A receipt,
blown crazily
across the parking lot,
was, perhaps,
a moth

Integer

1

One what?

One grasp?

No hands.

No collection

of stars. Something dark

pervades it.

2

Metaphor
is ritual sacrifice.

It kills the look-alike.

No,
metaphor is homeopathy.

A healthy cell
exhibits contact inhibition.

3

These temporary credits
will no longer be reflected
in your next billing period.

4

"Dark" meaning
not reflecting,

not amenable
to suggestion.

Report

What did the men look like?

I call 911 but reach a psychic hotline. All the service
numbers have been changed. Why wasn't I told? The
burglars sneer when I ask the psychic to "patch me
through" to the police. Chuck is searching for help
online but, of course, the screen freezes. We try joking
with the burglars about the telecomm system. They
laugh menacingly.

On the busy, patterned carpet,
one empty shoe nuzzles its twin.

Left

Shriveled hedge flowers
cast elaborate shadows

on the broad, bright, sharp
gladiola leaves

now?

If an instant
is a measure of

endurance,
what is the distance

from expectancy
to spider?

To get a small
constant,

we must wrap
many fluxes.

So says the

*

Left of zero,
a green colon blinks.

Somewhere a man yells,
"Move it!" "Jesus!"

We laugh.

In dreams, the words
speak themselves.

Several

1

Thus
drivers inching southward
will see the phalanx
of birds heading west
as one spontaneous
gesture.

2

We shrink from the old one
making her way
up the aisle
because her uncertainty
and her determination
are an unlikely pair,

or because her attention
has contracted
and she thinks nothing
of us,

or because she does not suggest
by smiling to herself
that this route
is only one
of several
imaginary paths.

Concentrate

The point at which
you can get
your eyelids to drift,

tethered,
like seaweed,

by thinking about it.
Then imagine yourself eyeless.

*

The spontaneity with which
a bubble breaks away,

flies to the surface
and pops

as if finding something out.

*

Now
in a vacuum

with virtuals
as probes

or as little
alarms
going off

Minimum Sum

1

Something like
a frilly tube worm

launched

what I want to call
a satellite

into what I
want to say

was "space"

to make it
sound familiar.

2

Undertone
means something's

in the room,
a blur of movement.

Stand still.

3

Let's pull back

from stipulation
to stipple.

Have done.

One of many
dull aches.

Once.

Lasting

1

Now light
sits in the chairs,

limns
the wooden

filigree

milled to indicate
leisure.

Perfect
molecules of plastic
sheet the seas.

2

When I remember my mother, I remember her fears.
But in the photograph, she leans on a pillar
hands in pockets, head cocked,
slightly amused.

Versions

1

So picture a virus
as a runaway

fragment,

a bit of living-dead
message —

"As if!"
perhaps, lost,

trolling for the warmth
it rejected.

It steals home
in the millions,

finds only
itself.

2

Jazz blown
across a patio,

each phrase

provisional,
self-satisfied

as the customers
almost are

The Light

The spread
of vicious talent contests
mimics the selection
of those best adapted
to the stage
of service industry capitalism.

*

One tells the story
of his illness
in such a way
as to make the others love him best.

*

Death is a smudge
on a film,

a spot
on the horizon.

*

We sleep together in the dark
but confuse
light with love.

*

In the televised moment,

a ruffled pink mantis
is snapping up vinegar flies.

Fade

The new reality
is a pastiche
of monologues.

Fighter pilots
in the Gulf

worry out loud
about their performance.

But how do *we*
come into it?

"Zombie Strippers!"

living pay-off
to pay-off,

numbed out,

avaricious

*

So much happiness
is caged
in language,

ready
to burst out
anytime

and fade

Take-Out

The feeling of emptiness

is a pre-existing condition.

Jargon

forces intimacy.

"I just called

to fill you in,"

      one says.

   *

Burger Lounge:

"What it means

to be grass-fed."

   *

If the patient cannot spin

background radiation

into context —

sick room,

white cube,

black box.

My remarks

are taken out of it.

Apartment

1

The woman on the mantel,
who doesn't much resemble me,
is holding a chainsaw
away from her body,
with a shocked smile,
while an undiscovered tumor
squats on her kidney.

2

The present
is a sentimental favorite,
with its heady mix
of grandiosity
and abjection,
truncated,
framed.

3

It's as if I'm subletting
a friend's apartment.
Even in the dream,
I'm trying to imagine
which friend.

And I'm trying to get
all my robes together,
robes I really own and
robes I don't

Remaining

1

It might be 1976. "Hotel California" is on every sound system. It tells us we're jaded — which is oddly terrific. This isn't going to take long at all. "Been there, done that," we will soon say. Tried to find the door. Futility features a soaring solo.

2

My parents are calling. "I Love Lucy" is about to start. It's funny the way Lucy wants to go too, do what Desi does. She wheedles and schemes. Her efforts, however, are not as impressive as Wile. E. Coyote's. When he fails, human ingenuity is foiled. Now Lucy is getting a laugh. She and Little Ricky can't open the door.

Still

Once we believed the bees,
moving as attention does,

settling and lifting
from blue identicals,

were the picture
of eternity.

*

Practiced hands knitting,
hole by hole,
a great, shapeless scarf.

Mind on something else.

*

A scarf?

Something intensive
seen from afar.

Something long

Hoop

God twirled
across the face of
what cannot be named
since it was not moving.

God was momentum then,
that impatience
with interruption,

stamping time's blanks
with its own image.

Now her theme will be
that she has escaped
certain destruction,

that she is
impossibly lucky.

This theme should be jaunty
but slightly discordant,

coming in, as it does,
so late.

The character
associated with this theme
should be dressed
in markedly old-fashioned clothing —

a hoop skirt perhaps —

while everyone else
is in cut-offs,

ready for the barbeque.

Anchor

"Widely expected,
if you will,
cataclysm."

Things I'd say,
am saying,

to persons no longer
present.

Yards away trim junipers
make their customary
bows.

"Oh, no thank you"
to any of it.

If you watch me
from increasing distance,

I am writing this
always

The Hole

A string of notes —

a string of words
could be a worm
or a needle

passing
in and out
through some hole —

stitching what to what?

I imagine myself
passing
among your thoughts,

a sleepwalker,

saying and doing things
I am ignorant of
as they occur.

Someone

1

I hear them talking
outside.

I know they're planning
to come in. They haven't

yet because they're waiting
for someone or something.

You might be amused by this.

(This focus on *out* and *in*.)

2

I'm looking for a
heart to heart,

a rhyme

between the blankness of my
"my"

and the blue emptiness

Only

Only the twins.

Positive and negative
"charges,"

push or pull
depending
on who's asking.

Who *is* asking?

*

"Should" says.

Now flowers lift
four-petal skirts,

obedient.

Thrown

1

She now carried out
both X,
which produced Y,
and Z,
which consumed it.

This seemed like completion.

So she broke herself
to bits,

but the sense
of having come full circle
could not be eliminated.

2

Medicine Shoppe,
Tear-Drop R.V.

Don't get cute with me!

The mind wanders.

The material
concentrates.

The whole plain
yellow
with bunchgrasses

across which
some loose flocks
are thrown

Pass

Single cells

become like-minded,

forming a consensus

or quorum.

Bioluminescence and virulence

are two ways

we describe the feeling

they share then.

With effort,

humans can approach

this condition.

"Synchronized swimming

has afforded me

a wonderful life,"

says one informant.

Why not?

I too would like

to exert power

over time,

to pass it,

aggressively, dramatically,

and forget all about it

until even

the meaning of the word

"pass"

gets lost

in a rosy glow.

Passage

I held the framework

of my life in mind

with some precision.

I knew when I was

where — or where I was

when — but not many

incidents of my past had

actually been preserved.

Instead the frame served

as a cargo cult runway,

forever inviting

the future to appear.

I existed finally

as the idea

of temporal extension.

2

The creeper
lineates
the wall.

Flowers as punctuation?

Can you elaborate
on the passage?

Double-meaning,

superposition:

hair standing on end

makes a creature appear
larger, more ferocious.

Fact

Operation Phantom Fury.

*

The full force
of the will to live
is fixed
on the next
occasion:

someone
coming with a tray,

someone
calling a number.

*

Each material
fact
is a pose,

an answer
waiting to be chosen.

"Just so," it says.

"Ask again!"

About the Author

Rae Armantrout is a professor of writing and literature at the University of California, San Diego, and the author of ten books of poetry.